STEAM'S LAMENT

London Midland Engine Sheds
Volume IV - 20A to 28B

Kevin Derrick

Strathwood

STEAM'S LAMENT

London Midland Engine Sheds
Volume IV - 20A to 28B

First published 2019
IISBN 978-1-905276-99-8

Copyright Strathwood Publishing 2019
Published by Strathwood Publishing, 9 Boswell Crescent, Inverness, IV2 3ET
Telephone 01463 234004
Printed by Akcent Media, Ltd.
www.strathwood.co.uk

Contents

20A Holbeck to 20E Manningham.. 4

21A Saltley to 21D Stratford-on-Avon... 27

22A Bristol Barrow Road to 22B Gloucester Barnwood.................................... 42

23A Skipton to 23C Lancaster 55

24A Accrington to 24D Lower Darwen.. 63

25A Wakefield to 25G Farnley Junction 76

26A Newton Heath to 26G Belle Vue 91

27A Bank Hall to 27E Walton-on-the-Hill..110

28A Blackpool Central to 28B Fleetwood...121

Page

This volume is compiled on the basis of the shed codes of 1948-1950 wherever possible

This Caprotti fitted Black Five was just a few weeks old when it caught the attention of our unknown cameraman on 24 July 1948, as it stood over the ash pits at 20A Leeds Holbeck. Instead of the programme of new Riddles designed Standard locomotives, British Railways could have carried on taking delivery of even more of the pre-nationalisation types than they actually did after 1948. Behind this somewhat uglier Ivatt version of Stanier's fine 4-6-0, is the large 300-ton double bunker coaler that dated from 1935 and the LMS. *www.TOPticl.com*

Our second view here at Holbeck was recorded just over ten years later on 23 August 1959 and depicts a British Railways Standard Class 9 from 21A Saltley with an equally filthy Standard Class 5MT in the background. Another factor from the intervening years here at Holbeck was the reduction of its allocation from almost one hundred locomotives down to eighty by 1959. *Colour Rail*

This Fowler Class 3F was a long term resident at Holbeck from 1948 until 1960, but in this view, it has lost its 20A shed plate whilst it awaits the new shed code 55A plate to be affixed, thus dating this view around February 1957. *Strathwood Library Collection*

Opposite: Another Holbeck regular was this Caprotti fitted Black Five, which was also fitted with Timken roller bearings and a double chimney. Looking unloved it has been fitted with the new 55A shed code when seen around the same time on shed. *Strathwood Library Collection*

There were two roundhouses here at Holbeck with the now sadly nameless Britannia 70034 Thomas Hardy trying to shelter from the rain in one of the two entrances to the No.1 Roundhouse on 7 October 1966.
Strathwood Library Collection

Opposite: Transferred into the Eastern Region after 3 February 1957 as 55A Holbeck continued to retain its flavour as an ex-Midland Railway shed, even after its last two 4-4-0s were transferred away in 1960. Receiving instructions from the yard foreman the driver of this Hughes/Fowler Crab from 24J Lancaster shunts the Black Five up to the coaler in 1960.
Strathwood Library Collection

Right: Inside the No.2 Roundhouse at Holbeck on 29 September 1961, another form of Caprotti fitted Class 5MT in the shape of this Standard, Riddles designed version 73129 from Patricroft. After withdrawal in December 1967, thanks to being purchased as scrap by Dai Woodham it has since joined the ranks of the preservation movement.
Rail Online

The second view of Britannia Pacific 70034 Thomas Hardy is looking into the No.1 Roundhouse at Holbeck on 7 October 1966.
Strathwood Library Collection & Bill Wright

Opposite: By November 1967, diesels outnumbered steam at Holbeck and the dignity of shed plates and cylinder covers was something of the past for this Class 9F visiting from Birkenhead just days before being withdrawn and for Holbeck being closed to steam.
Colour Rail

Before we take our leave of Holbeck a return to happier times on 29 September 1961 just prior to the real diesel invasion that was on the horizon with one of Holbeck's own Britannias 70054 Dornoch Firth being prepared to come off shed. *Rail Online*

While Holbeck was more of the passenger locomotive shed for the Leeds area the former Midland Railway chose Stourton as their shed for freight workings. Taking water by the coal stage at Stourton in September 1966 was 43044 just one of several Ivatt Class 4MTs on shed that day. *Colour Rail*

Left: The roundhouse was rebuilt at the start of the fifties as seen behind Class 3F 47538 on 25 May 1952 whilst still coded 20B. The shed code became 55B on 3 February 1957 and closed to steam on 15 January 1967. **Strathwood Library Collection**

Four Stanier Class 8Fs await a recall to service from their slumber at Stourton on Sunday 26 June 1966, the wheels on 48311 look to be rusty so she may have been set aside a while beforehand, although not withdrawn for a couple more months yet. **Rail Online**

Two views of Royston one on a weekday in 1960 and the second on Saturday 20 May 1967. **Photos: Strathwood Library Collection & Jerry Beddows**

This Johnson Class 1P 0-4-4 was built by Dubs & Co. for the Midland Railway in 1892 and still showed the BRITISH RAILWAYS lettering beneath the paint and grime from when it was first renumbered in July 1949 in this scene on shed at Royston taken on 24 June 1956.
Eric Sawford/The Transport Treasury

Opposite: Royston shed remained as 20C until 3 February 1957 when it became 55D, being closed to steam on 4 November 1967 although it was still open to diesels until 26 September 1971. On 29 September 1961, Jubilee 45716 Swiftsure was visiting from 12A Carlisle Kingmoor.
Rail Online

Contrasts at Normanton with members of our coach party heading towards the ex-Lancashire & Yorkshire Railway shed here in February 1967. To the left of the cinder path from the road bridge, Standard Class 3MT Moguls 77004, 77003 & 77000 all await their fate. *Rail Photoprints*

Opposite: Taken from a similar spot during the 'great freeze' of 1963 a lonesome footplateman comes off shift past a line up of stone cold Austerities, a Crab and a Fowler Class 4F all in winter storage, but with the prospect of seeing action once more. *Strathwood Library Collection*

A few more younger spotters make their way towards the shed at Normanton on 31 July 1967, they look like they would not have known the shed when it was coded 20D up until 3 February 1957, they were about to witness its closure though which came on 5 November 1967 whilst as 55E within the Eastern Region. *The Transport Treasury*

Opposite: At the start of the fifties as 20D Normanton boasted almost twenty Stanier Class 8F 2-8-0s as part of its allocation, once within the Eastern Region's boundaries these were replaced with around fifteen Austerities just like this visitor 90044 on shed today from 50B Hull Dairycoates on 22 August 1965. *Strathwood Library Collection*

Normanton also found work for this LMS Derby built Fowler Class 2P throughout the fifties until 40630 seen here on 28 April 1957 by the former Lancashire & Yorkshire Railway's 'coal hole' until it was withdrawn in October 1960. *Colour Rail*

Opposite: A late arrival to Normanton was this Austerity 90721 after being re-allocated here in September 1966, she was to be seen moving away from the newer mechanical coaler and underneath the ashplant on 28 March 1967. *Rail Photoprints*

Opposite: In the last week of steam here at Normanton during November 1967, these three footplatemen share a chuckle as they make their way off duty as the sounds of diesel engines now compete with Black Five 45209 from 10A Carnforth starting to blow off in the background. *Colour Rail*

The once large ex-Midland Railway's shed at 20E Bradford Manningham was one less visited by cameramen of the day. Its allocation almost halved during the fifties as DMUs arrived in the area. On 22 May 1955, this Fairburn Class 4MT was just five years into traffic as it made its way towards the roundhouse past the 'coal hole'. *Rail Online*

Old habits seemed to die hard at Manningham as we can see not only the large roundhouse in the background to this 7 May 1961 view but also a reasonable number of locomotives still being stabled on the roads of the original four-road wooden shed that had disappeared during the war years. Another view taken the same day found this home allocated Fairburn Class 4MT stabled between the shed yard and the adjacent station. The shed at Manningham closed as 55E on 29 April 1967.
Both: Strathwood Library Collection

Above: A panoramic view of Saltley taken around 1962 shows how the then new Peak diesels were being segregated from steam. There were two further roundhouses behind the No.3 Roundhouse we are facing toward. In the early fifties, Saltley then coded as 21A held the biggest allocation of locomotives on the London Midland Region with just over one hundred and ninety examples on its books. *Colour Rail*

The rebuilding of the former Midland Railway's roundhouses was still being carried out when this view was taken on 28 March 1954 of this Johnson Class 2F stabled on its home shed here at 21A Saltley. *Strathwood Library Collection*

A fine line up of all three of the Standard Class 9Fs that were fitted with Berkeley mechanical stokers at Saltley in 1962 as part of the shed's large allocation of freight engines still engaged on moving much of what Birmingham's then still busy factories were producing. *The Transport Treasury*

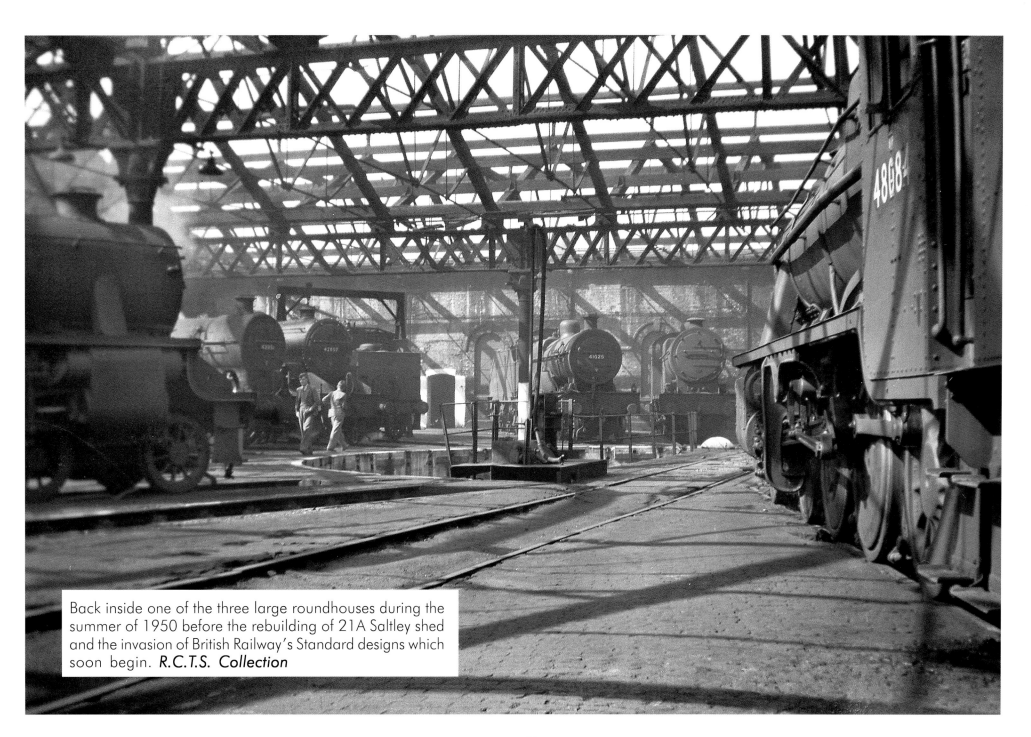

Back inside one of the three large roundhouses during the summer of 1950 before the rebuilding of 21A Saltley shed and the invasion of British Railway's Standard designs which soon begin. *R.C.T.S. Collection*

The shed code had changed to 2E for Saltley on 9 September 1963, when we visited in late 1966 steam activity was almost at a close for these three Standard Class 9Fs basking in the sunshine streaming in through the rebuilt roof. *Brian Robbins/Rail Photoprints*

Opposite: On 25 June 1951 with the new roof still to be built above we can see how shed life was for a while as the unique and ugly stove-pipe chimney fitted Ivatt Class 4MT 43027 was almost ready for the turntable to be made ready to move off shed. *Rail Photoprints*

Opposite: As late as 1959 there were still in excess of one hundred and seventy steam locomotives allocated to 21A Saltley. Although the numbers of ex-Midland Railway designs had declined in favour of nineteen Standard Class 9Fs including 92137 seen here on 29 July 1961. This powerful 2-10-0 had arrived when new in June 1957 and would remain allocated to Saltley until sent away to 6C Croes Newydd in August 1966. *Colour Rail*

Black Five 45447 enjoyed two spells as a Saltley locomotive, the first from 1948 until 1953, then again from 1959 until 1965. Therefore she was no stranger here when recorded on 16 June 1962, although the fact she still carried her early British Railways emblem caught our photographer's attention. *R.C.T.S. Collection*

Not all of the turns dealt with by Saltley were freight of course, they also enjoyed the likes of Royal Scot 46118 Royal Welch Fusilier as part of their allocation when visited on 6 May 1962. Although the arrival of Peak Class diesels would see this fine 4-6-0 re-allocated away the following month to 12B Carlisle Upperby. *Ian Turnbull/Rail Photoprints*

Opposite: There seems to be an abundance of fire irons propped up against the buffer stop to the side of Saltley's Johnson Class 3F 43521 engaged on shed pilot duties on 22 July 1961. There had formally been three sub-sheds to Saltley at Camp Hill, Kingsbury and Water Orton but these had already been closed by this time. *The Transport Treasury*

The ex-Midland Railway shed at Bourneville coded 21B was once described as a quiet backwater retirement home for elderly engines. It was left as a working museum to some extent after the war and this was the scene inside the roundhouse on 5 April 1958. The transfer of its duties to Saltley and Bromsgrove saw 21B Bourneville closed on 15 February 1960. On this date its sub-shed at Redditch which is seen here with Fowler Class 4MT 42334 and two Johnson Class 2F stabled within became a sub-shed to 21C Bromsgrove instead. *Both: Strathwood Library Collection*

Bromsgrove shed may have only enjoyed a small allocation but every railway enthusiast knew what they were there for as banking engines for the 1 in 37 Lickey Incline. The shed was established here from the very start of the Midland Railway's route into the Lickey Hills in 1840. At nationalization the shed retained the shed code of 21C, however, on 1 February 1958, it was moved within the Western Region under Worcester shed as 85F. Then on 1 January 1961 Bromsgrove shed took over the former Kidderminster shed code of 85D which it would keep up until closure on 26 September 1964. Bromsgrove enjoyed three dedicated 'super bankers' during the British Railways era, the most famous of which was the purpose designed 0-10-0 affectionately known as Big Bertha seen overleaf whilst waiting at the coaling stage at the foot of the climb in October 1953. Withdrawal came for Big Bertha in May 1956 when her boiler was condemned after many years of hard work mixed with longer periods waiting here at the bottom of the climb. Her eventual replacement was Standard Class 9F 92079 which also inherited the large headlight from Big Bertha. The Western Region allocated several of its Hawksworth 94xx panniers to release most of the Fowler Class 3F Jinties back to the London Midland Region after 1958. *Photos: Strathwood Library Collection & Rail Photoprints*

Our next 'super banker' for the Lickey came about more by accident being a former LNER locomotive this Class U1 69999 had originally been purchased in 1925 as a banking engine for the 1 in 40 Worsborough Incline between Wentworth Junction and West Silkstone near Barnsley. From March 1949 until November 1950 this leviathan was used on the Lickey and based here at Bromsgrove where we see her in May 1949. Perhaps because this was a steeper grade with the locomotive being pushed to its limits, those limits were proving to be beyond the capabilities of a single fireman to keep such a large grate adequately fed, this was after all the largest and most powerful steam engine to be employed on British Railways. It was then returned to Mexborough shed until July 1955 when it was given another go as a possible longer-term replacement for Big Bertha. As a result, 69999 was converted to burn oil to overcome the firing issues, this also meant the use of the diminutive ex-Caledonian Railway Drummond Class 0F 56020 to act as the heating and pumping engine for 69999's oil supply. The whole idea was set aside in favour of the dedicated Class 9F 92079 in May 1956. *Frank Hornby/The Transport Treasury*

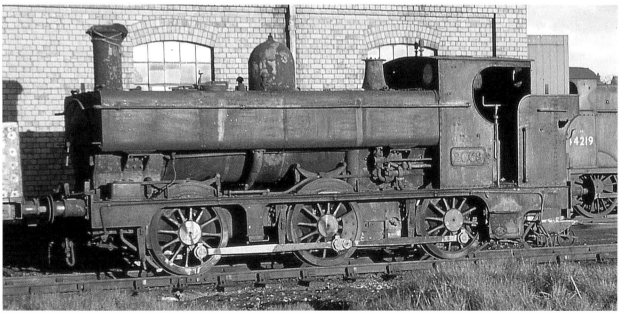

Ultimately absorbed within the LMS, the former Stratford-on-Avon & Midland Junction Railway's shed was coded as 21D Stratford-on-Avon as the nationalized railway took control in 1948. It seems Fowler Class 4F 44219 was a regular here as it appears in these two views firstly on 26 August 1955, and once again in the background to the stored and withdrawn Dean Class 2021 0-6-0PT 2069 on 8 April 1959.
Photos: Strathwood Library Collection & Gerald T. Robinson

A second view taken on 26 August 1955 at 21D Stratford-on-Avon yields 22B Gloucester Barnwood's, Johnson Class 3F 43258. In February 1953, Stratford-on-Avon's shed had lost its own allocation code and became just a sub-shed to 21A Saltley. *Strathwood Library Collection*

Opposite: The city of Bristol boasted three large engine sheds during the British Railway's steam era with the former Midland Railway's establishment coded 22A Barrow Road retaining an allocation of around fifty to sixty locomotives throughout the fifties. Around ten Stanier Jubilees were allocated here for working expresses towards the Midlands, among their number was 45690 Leander which aside from a couple of weeks based supposedly at 89A Shrewsbury in September 1961, this fine locomotive remained a Barrow Road Jubilee right up until withdrawal in March 1964. This elevated view looking towards the roundhouse from the Barrow Road bridge is from around 1959. *Rail Photoprints*

This Black Five's only association with Bristol Barrow Road through the years would have been for servicing whilst visiting the city. Certainly by early 1965 when this shot was taken, steam activity at both Bath Road and St. Phillip's Marsh had already ceased as the Western Region strove to be steam-free. Servicing for steam ended here at Barrow Road on 21 November 1965.
Strathwood Library Collection

The driver of Stanier Class 8F 48253 gazes across to rows of withdrawn Western Region Panniers at Barrow Road as they await their passage to South Wales scrap dealers on 3 July 1965. *Rail Photoprints*

The Western Region had assumed control of Bristol Barrow Road as 82E since 1 February 1958, therefore, 7926 Willey Hall might have been a regular here in her last year of service during 1964. *Rail Online*

Many cameramen of the day were tempted to make full use of the elevated views provided from the Barrow Road bridge while visiting the shed as here with a clean looking Class 8F 48609 or perhaps a full looking yard on Tuesday 31 October 1961. *Photos: Strathwood Library Collection & Rail Photoprints*

This looks like another good turn out in the yard for these spotters at Gloucester Barnwood in July 1963. As another ex-Midland Railway shed it had joined British Railways coded 22B in 1948, a code it would maintain up until 1 February 1958 when it joined the Western Region as 85E. Then on 1 January 1961, it assumed the code of 85C which had been previously Hereford, until Barnwood's closure on 8 May 1964. *Colour Rail*

Opposite: The main shed building was the large roundhouse supported by the usual fitting shop and a traditional style of coaling stage which is seen behind these two visiting Black Fives, with 44852 from 55A Holbeck and 45272 in from 21A Saltley on 3 November 1962. When Barnwood closed in 1964 its remaining locomotives and staff transferred to the nearby 85B Gloucester Horton Road shed. *Peter Simmonds*

Opposite: A facility that would be used in coming years by the Western Region for its own locomotives too was the wheel drop here at Barnwood, as the fitters attend to the needs of home allocated Johnson Class 1F 41720 approaching the end of its life when photographed on 24 August 1955. *Strathwood Library Collection*

After spending some time in open storage here at Barnwood this duo of Fowler Class 3F Jinties would see further use after this view, taken on 6 September 1963, as they were both transferred to 82F Bath Green Park that November where they found another four months of work for themselves. *Rail Photoprints*

East meets West in the yard at Gloucester Barnwood on 3 November 1962 with the arrival to the city of this Gresley Class K3 61853 in from 56B Ardsley. *Peter Simmonds*

Barnwood boasted two sub-sheds one at Dursley and one here at Tewkesbury with time for some conversation perhaps about the shed's damaged water crane on 12 August 1961.
R.C.T.S Collection

In earlier days there was a cast iron lamp post appointed to illuminate the water column by the shed at Tewkesbury with 58071 a Johnson Class 2P in from the parent shed at Barnwood on this occasion. The rather basic coaling facilities here can be seen on 19 April 1958 with both the Johnson Class 3F 43520 or Ivatt Class 4MT 43049 unlikely to be re-coaled manually unless their needs were dire! These facilities closed on 29 September 1962.
Both: Strathwood Library Collection

Opposite: Skipton's previously rundown ex-Midland Railway shed was rebuilt in this form by British Railways in the early fifties with a variety of locomotive types still visible in September 1963.
Eric Sawford/The Transport Treasury

Opposite & Right: Around 1966 there was this mass gathering of redundant Fowler Class 4Fs, some fitted for snow plough duties at Skipton to await their disposal. Coded as 23A after 1950, it had been 20F since nationalization. It would undergo further changes, back to 20F in 1951. Then 24G from 1957 until 1963 when it adopted 10G until it closed completely on 3 April 1967. On 17 June 1966 things still looked okay for this Ivatt and Stanier combo. *Both: Strathwood Library Collection*

Below: By the British Railway's era Keighley shed had become a sub-shed of Skipton, although in the Midland Railway's days it was under Manningham, closure for Keighley shed came on 18 June 1962.
Strathwood Library Collection

Likewise the code changes would come thick and fast for Hellifield starting as 20G in 1948, then 23B from 1950 until 1951, back to 20G until 1957, then 24H for its last years until closure on 17 June 1963. Happier times with a clean looking Jubilee 45607 Fiji in 1956 contrasts with a grubby Black Five 44662 in the shed's final year.

Photos: Rail Photoprints & Strathwood Library Collection

Tucked around the back of the running shed at Hellifield next to the turntable on 4 September 1955 was Stanier Class 8F 48616 proudly wearing its 20G allocation plate on its home shed. Although the shed was overlooked by the fells, it once supported considerable goods traffic which was marshalled and sorted in both of Hellifield's yards. The footplate crew of this work stained Hughes/Fowler Crab take it easy before moving off shed here in 1962.
Both: Strathwood Library Collection

Opposite: The Midland Railway met up with the LNWR at Lancaster, with the former building their shed at Green Ayre on the south bank of the River Lune. The gantries in the background to this shot of Ivatt Class 2MT 41221 acting as shed pilot here around 1961 were for the later aborted 1500v dc EMU service to Morecambe and Heysham from Lancaster Green Ayre.
Rail Online

Carrying the rather rare shed code plate for collectors of 11E as Lancaster Green Ayre in 1952 was Stanier Class 2P 41900. The shed codes for Green Ayre made numerous changes, starting with 20H from nationalization until 1950, then 23C for a year, before becoming 11E as seen above until 1957. Then it would be changed again to 24J under Accrington to close finally in 1966 under Carnforth having been 10J after 1963.
Strathwood Library Collection

Opposite: The future looks grim now for both 41903 and 41904 sacked up at Lancaster Green Ayre on 25 February 1961 as both of these Stanier Class 2Ps had been withdrawn since November 1959.
Strathwood Library Collection

The importance of the steam shed at Accrington coded 24A fell away fast by the close of the fifties as it was converted to handle DMU maintenance, as a result, it seems the photographers of the time followed 24A's locomotives and men to 24B Rose Grove after 6 March 1961. On shed in 1957 at Accrington was this Aspinall Class 2F in its last year here. Whereas photographs of of Rose Grove in its last days during 1968 are almost commonplace as enthusiasts recorded all they could.
Photos: Strathwood Library Collection & Dave Livesey

On 2 August 1968, we see what was almost certainly the last steam derailment of the British Railway's standard gauge era, when this Class 8F picked the points coming on shed at Rose Grove. This meant 48666 was not fit for the final Sunday's end of steam railtour from Blackburn to Carnforth, with 48773 to the left taking its place. *Strathwood Library Collection*

Shed bashing by the summer of 1968 for many became concentrated on the last few steam sheds to remain open. Many photographers having taken their summer holidays from work specifically to record these scenes for posterity. This was Black Five 45287 having its smokebox cleaned out on Wednesday 3 July 1968. Any considerations to maintaining previously tidiness and safety standards around the coaler have obviously gone to pot here at Rose Grove. *Jerry Beddows*

Aside from the famed footplate cameraman Jim Carter very few photographers dared to climb up onto either the shed's coaler or ashplant to bring us elevated views sadly from the age of steam. However, by 21 July 1968, there were few shed staff left to send you packing if you went for a view such as this of the ex-War Department Stanier 8F 48775 with its larger top feed as it makes its way through the coaling road. *Jerry Beddows*

Opposite: This was the view looking across the front of the shed yard the same day with nine of Stanier's finest all coaled up and ready to go in the summer sunshine on this quiet Sunday lunchtime at Rose Grove. *Jerry Beddows*

In September 1965 the role of shed pilot at Lostock hall was still very much in the hands of steam with this home allocated Jinty doing the honours today. Lostock Hall was another shed that became almost open house during 1968 in the last year of steam as it found itself the focus of almost every spotter's attentions, also being conveniently located next to the station. *Rail Online*

This youngster in his duffle coat and other visitors are on hand during April 1968 to witness this Black Five having its fire cleaned.at Lostock Hall in surroundings that appear certainly tidier than those, we have just seen at nearby Rose Grove.
Strathwood Library Collection

Having been coded as 24C since nationalization Lostock Hall would start to see some changes including the likes of the now-withdrawn Patriot 45505 The Royal Army Ordnance Corps and one of its own Jintys awaiting their destiny and the creation of a scrap road at the shed when visited on 17 July 1962. *Strathwood Library Collection*

Among the changes during the sixties here at Lostock Hall was the change of the shed code to 10D on 9 September 1963. Changes included the loss of around sixteen Austerity 2-8-0s to be replaced by Stanier Class 8Fs instead to work some of the shed's freight turns. On 28 February 1968 there is a small gathering around Black Five 45345 whereas 48253 reflects upon past glories. *Colour Rail*

The writing was already on the wall when Lostock Hall was visited on 24 June 1968, once again everything still looked tidy all around even with closure on 5 August approaching fast.
Bill Wright

The lifeless 47002 has to be dragged about Lostock Hall by a recently arrived diesel shunter on 11 June 1962, however, the valiant little 0-4-0ST still has another two years service here to look forward to.
Strathwood Library Collection

Perhaps it was the forty-five minutes walking time from the nearest station that put visitors off from 24D Lower Darwen as it is certainly less well photographed than many other ex-Lancashire & Yorkshire Railway sheds on the region. A visit on Saturday 18 June 1961 rewards us with Standard Class 4MT Mogul 76084 back on its then home shed. The shed code would change along with so many others on 9 February 1963, in this case, to become 10H. Our next visit on 1 May 1965 provides further clues to the mainly freight nature of Lower Darwen as DMUs were now in charge of local passengers duties. The shed succumbed to closure on St. Valentine's day 1966. *Photos: David T. Williams & Strathwood Library Collection*

Following the ex-Lancashire & Yorkshire Railway, we arrive at 25A Wakefield in 1953 and an obvious Eastern influence with Classes J50 and J39 to greet us, along with one of the named Thompson Class B1s 60129 Chamois on 25 February 1965. **Both: Strathwood Library Collection**

Opposite: As might be expected Wakefield shed found itself drawn within Eastern Region control as 56A after September 1956. One of the step-sided tender fitted Class V2s was on shed on 29 September five years later. As steam gave way to diesels here after 1964, the shed finally closed on 25 June 1967 as activity then centred upon Healey Mills diesel depot. *Rail Online*

The former London & North Western Railway forged their interests into Yorkshire by establishing a shed at Huddersfield Hillhouse which continued as 25B after nationalization. Just like Wakefield and the remaining sheds coded in the 25 series, Huddersfield Hillhouse was absorbed within the Eastern Region, in this case as 55G but a little later on 3 February 1957. A visit to the shed on 22 June 1961 found it still with very much with a London Midland Region appearance. As a mainly a freight and local passenger shed its largest allocated class were Austerity 2-8-0s such as 90621 seen taking a breather here in 1964. *Both: Strathwood Library Collection*

Soon after Huddersfield Hillhouse became 55G within the Eastern Region we find Fowler Class 4MT 42409 as part of a large Sunday turnout at the shed on 28 April 1957. The Eastern Region finally had their way and closed the shed on 1 January 1967. *Colour Rail*

Opposite & This Page: Supplying shunters for the dockyard at Goole meant that several of these ex-Lancashire & Yorkshire Railway 'Pugs' were retained throughout the fifties here at 25C. In 1956 the shed became 53E and as part of the Eastern Region the numbers of Austerities here began to increase as a result. Another code change came in 1960 making it 50D. Steam ceased here on 25 June 1967, but diesels continued to use the shed until 4 February 1973.

Photos: Strathwood Library Collection

Mirfield shed through the years as its seen firstly still as 25D on 13 May 1956, then a wider view in 1961 after its change to 56D. Finally on this page with two shots from 1966 before final closure to steam on 2 January 1967.

Photos: Strathwood Library Collection & Jim Winkley

Sowerby Bridge was another ex-Lancashire & Yorkshire Railway shed that became a backwater seldom visited by photographers of the fifties and sixties. As 25F Sowerby Bridge enjoyed an allocation of just over thirty locomotives at the start of the fifties which had only fallen to twenty-six by the start fo the next decade. It proved to be a stronghold for a number of the old company's survivors including this Aspinall Class 3F 52515 in steam here on 20 July 1962 during its last year of service.
Strathwood Library Collection

Opposite: Newer designs came and went such as this Ivatt Class 2MT Mogul 46438 in what appears to be unlined black and wearing larger cab numerals when recorded on 29 September 1961 at Sowerby Bridge. In the shed's final year before closure on 11 January 1964, the allocation was made up from nine somewhat life expired Austerity 2-8-0s. **Rail Online**

Low Moor shed near Bradford was developed from early Lancashire & Yorkshire Railway days into a large twelve-road shed coded as 25F up until September 1956, when it joined the Eastern Region as 56F. On 22 July 1967 just before closure, Black Five 44694 reverses past the original 'coal hole' towards the LMS installed mechanical replacement from the thirties. *Gerald T. Robinson*

Opposite: A healthy allocation of Fairburn Class 4MTs were allocated here at Low Moor from nationalization to almost the last days at the shed. Giving some clues as to what it was like overnight between duties at Low Moor on 8 October 1966 as the mist, smoke and steam make photography challenging we find 42116. **Strathwood Library Collection**

This Page & Opposite: Farnley Junction as 25G became 55C in 1956 as all of these West Riding sheds under Wakefield joined the Eastern Region. It had originally been a London & North Western Railway shed constructed within the triangle of lines from Dewsbury, Heckmondwick and Farnley & Wortley. The Shed directory of the day suggested that Farnley Junction shed was fifty-five minutes walking time from Leeds City station which might have put many spotters off making their way there. Aside from a few Jubilees and Black Fives, the bulk of its allocation was made up during the fifties with over twenty Austerity 2-8-0s. So the appearance of this Britannia in 1967, albeit complete with a buckled frame, in un-lined green and painted nameplate was by way of perhaps a late treat. Although not a patch on an earlier visit with 45578 United Provinces about to lead two fellow Jubilees off shed on 22 February 1963. *Photos: Jim Winkley & Rail Online*

Opposite: Secreted away in a corner of Farnley Junction on 22 February 1963 was 46145 The Duke of Wellington's Regt. (West Riding) one of several withdrawn Royal Scots dumped here around this time. It had turned up here a few months beforehand during December 1962. It was put back into steam on 23 September 1963 in order that it could haul 46103 Royal Scots Fusilier and 46130 The West Yorkshire Regiment away from here for the trio to be scrapped at Crewe Works.
Strathwood Library Collection

Newton Heath was the major Lancashire & Yorkshire Railway's engine shed for Manchester with what had previously been a huge twenty-four through road steam shed which had held the code of 26A from 1948 until 1963 when it became 9D. By the time of this view on 30 April 1966, the south side of the shed had been pulled down to make way for a new servicing shed for diesel locomotives and multiple units. **Colour Rail**

Opposite: At the start of the fifties, Newton Heath shed boasted in excess of one-hundred and sixty locomotives including ten Jubilees among its allocation. By the time of this view in 1963 with a filthy 45716 Swiftsure now bereft of its nameplates running up the shed yard, Newton Heath's allocation had halved. **Rail Photoprints**

The distinctive style of ex-Lancashire & Yorkshire Railway water column stands proudly alongside, as the fireman of a cleaned up Black Five and Standard Class 4MT 75019 are being watered and prepared for their rail tour duties in 1968 away from Newton Heath, steam activity came to an end here on 1 July in this year.
Strathwood Library Collection

A different style of water column dominates the scene of this 6H Bangor allocated Fowler Class 4F visiting Newton Heath around 1960. *Rail Photoprints*

Opposite: On 22 August 1959, a fine collection of motorcycles stand alongside this fully coaled Crab at Newton Heath, the fact that two carry L plates suggest they belong to young firemen. *Colour Rail*

It looks to be a cold day as 26B Agecroft's long-standing Jinty 47579 simmers away nicely as do the braziers to keep yet another style of water column from freezing up around the turn of the sixties. The shed took on the code of 9J after 9 September 1963 which saw it through to closure on 17 October 1966. *Rail Online*

Opposite: Subsidence from the nearby Agecroft Colliery caused many problems for the railway and the shed buildings through the years. On 21 June 1961, this Thompson Class B1 61008 Kudu was midway through a two and half year spell of being allocated here at 26B Agecroft. *Colour Rail*

The last operational Fowler Class 7F 49508 was withdrawn from here at Agecroft on 20 January 1962, around a year beforehand this same locomotive was recorded being shunted to a new position within the shed yard by Jinty 47546 from 26A Newton Heath. Ultimately this once mighty Fowler 0-8-0 would be dispatched to Crewe Works for disposal within the Melts Shop in early 1962. *Strathwood Library Collection*

It's a rainy day in 1968 and steam traction and a whole way of life is coming to an end for this footplateman strolling away from these three Stanier Class 8Fs at Bolton shed. *Dave Livesey*

Opposite: The LMS made a number of improvements to Bolton shed during the mid-thirties which included new coaling and ash disposal facilities, although the old Lancashire & Yorkshire Railway's 'coal hole' remained to supply water and for additional shelter. When this Black Five was being attended in the spring of 1968 the shed was now coded as 9K and would be soon to close on the first day of July. *Dave Livesey*

No such thoughts would be going through the mind of this footplateman taking a breather whilst disposing of Stanier Class 8F 48113 from 20C Royston alongside the 26C Bolton coaler on 9 August 1953. The shed's fortunes were bolstered the following year when the duties from tthe own's other shed at Plodder Lane came across when it was closed that October. *The Transport Treasury*

Opposite: Having come in from 27B Aintree, this Hughes/Fowler Crab is being brought gently up to the water column to quench its thirst at Bolton on 23 April 1960. It would find itself transferred here to Bolton in May 1963 to work its final three months before being withdrawn. **Colour Rail**

A harsh movement of the regulator has put Black Five 45260 into a violent slip whilst being moved away from the coaler and alongside the old 'coal hole' on a bitterly cold February day in early 1968 at Bolton. **Dave Livesey**

The ex-Lancashire & Yorkshire Railway's shed here at Bury kept its LMS coding of 26D until 1963 when it became 9M. The initial electrification of the Manchester to Bury line in 1916 took away a number of duties for the shed even before LMS days. One of the second generation EMUs introduced by British Railways rolls past the shed in October 1964. The shed would close officially six months later, however, it was used to store an array of AC and DC electric locomotives from 1967 until 1972. *Both: Colour Rail*

It was the closure of 26E Bacup in October 1954 and the transfer of its duties to Bury that perhaps helped keep the latter going as long as it did. The early closure and backwater nature for yet another ex-Lancashire & Yorkshire railway shed kept it out of the limelight for cameramen. Although it lasted long enough to be visited by several British Railways Standards such as this almost new Class 3MT 84017 from Bury on 23 April 1954 and a Class 4MT in the middle in our second shot taken just before closure. *Both: **Strathwood Library Collection***

Lees in Oldham was an ex-London & North Western Railway outpost coded 26F up until 1955 when it took over as 26E from the recently closed Bacup. The shed was rebuilt as we can see between 1949 in our first view and the second around ten years later. *Both: Strathwood Library Collection*

This duo of Aspinall Class 3Fs had just been withdrawn and set aside alongside the shed to be made ready for their last journey to the breakers when seen on 11 November 1962. The following year Lees shed was recoded again as 9P, which it held for its last six months of existence until 13 April 1964. *Rail Online*

Left: The removal of the packed in snow and ice choking one of the access points into Lees shed once again during the fifties has brought out a 'spare gang' and one of the shed's Austerities armed with a steam lance to get things on the move again. *Strathwood Library Collection*

A late season snowfall in 1954 across Oldham finds a motor-fitted Fowler Class 3MT still in the shed yard rather than working the 'Delph Donkey' this morning. *Colour Rail*

The ex-Midland Railway shed at Belle Vue was another overlooked by visitors and cameramen alike, code changes abounded from 19E in 1948, through 13B, 26G to finally 26F for its last six-months before closure on 16 April 1956.
Strathwood Library Collection

Opposite & Above: Bank Hall was the principle shed for the Lancashire & Yorkshire Railway in Liverpool starting out as 23A at nationalisation, it became 27A from 1950 through until 1963 when the shed code of 8K was adopted. The shed's entrance was opposite Bank Hall station with the shed directory suggesting all visitors had to do was cross Stanley Road and enter the shed via the offices. There it seems was the problem in some circles as a legend among some spotters suggest the shed foreman was not happy about unofficial visitors. However, these two cameramen made it around safely firstly on 17 October 1966 which was the shed's last day. Whereas a previous visit in the fifties saw the shed roof in a better state of repair when photographing this Fowler Class 4MT in the yard.

Photos: Strathwood Library Collection & Colour Rail

The Lancashire & Yorkshire Railway established some extensive sorting sidings for their freight traffic at Aintree requiring a large shed to service the required locomotives. This once busy shed was much improved and capable of everyday servicing of Standard Class 9Fs such as 92157 and opposite Royal Scot 46125 3rd Carabinier, which would have been just one of a large number locomotives here for Grand National Day on 30 March 1963. The shed was coded 23B, then 27B and finally 8L when seen below on closure day 12 June 1967.

Photos: Strathwood Library Collection & Rail Photoprints

Opposite: When British Railways inherited the ex-Lancashire & Yorkshire Railway shed at Southport in 1948, the LMS had made a start on repairing the shed roof, albeit it seems badly as can be seen behind Stanier Class 3MT 40190 affording very little shelter to the locomotives including one of Southport's five new Standard Class 4MTs in May 1954. *Colour Rail*

Shed codes came and went from 23C, 27C to finally 8M at closure on 6 June 1966. The later aborted preservation scheme as Steamport took over the site, but due to decay and costs, it closed at the turn of the Millenium. Recalling happier days on 2 March 1960 we see a Stanier Class 4MT taking coal on its home shed. *Alec Swain/The Transport Treasury*

Opposite: A batch of five of these Standard Class 2MT Moguls were sent new to 27D Wigan L&Y in the autumn of 1956 to help replace many of the old company's locomotives. *Rail Online*

The decrepit state of the former Lancashire & Yorkshire Railway's shed at 27D Wigan L&Y can be judged below before it was recladded in the mid-fifties. The shed was also known as Prescott Street or Central amongst the men. It was re-coded as 8P in September 1963 before closure on 13 April 1964.
Photos: Strathwood Library Collection & Rail Online

The side roads of the shed at 27D Wigan had once been undercover too before the buildings were cut back to scrimp on repairs and were later used for locomotive and wagon storage as here with an ex-LNWR 0-8-0 from Springs Branch in the late fifties. *Rail Online*

The former Cheshire Lines shed at Walton-on-the-Hill was originally coded as 13F becoming 27E from 1949 until 1963. Rarely visited it seems, it had a Class K3 and a fairly new Thompson Class B1 still numbered as E1288 when recorded around 1949. The flavour was much more in keeping with a London Midland Region shed code for this next view on Sunday 21 July 1957. *Both: Strathwood Library Collection*

These two former Great Central Railway Class J10s in storage within what was left of the roof structure at Walton on 10 September 1950, seem unlikely to see much use if any again, as certainly 65130 was withdrawn in August 1952, whereas 65128 behind was withdrawn just a few weeks after this shot was taken.
Peter Pescod/The Transport Treasury

There were two sheds located in Blackpool by the Lancashire & Yorkshire Railway, with the main shed here at Blackpool Central. The smaller shed was known as Talbot Road or Blackpool North, although they both enjoyed the same shed codes. Starting within the British Railway's era as 24E, then to 28A and back again to 24E all before 1 April 1952. Things settled down as the last change came on 9 September 1963 to 10B before closing on 10 February 1964. It seems Talbot Road or Blackpool North opened for a while as stabling point in March 1966. This was the view towards Blackpool Central overlooking the empty tourist coach car park on a rather sunny but brisk 26 February 1963. *Strathwood Library Collection*

Both of Blackpool's sheds were rebuilt by British Railways as late as 1957/8 even though dieselization was already on the march as here with a DMU car visible to the right of the Black Five and Ivatt Class 4MT on 20 April 1961. *Rail Online*

Jubilees on shed at Blackpool Central firstly with 45681 Aboukir on 6 September 1962. Secondly with 45675 Hardy on 22 September 1963.
Photos Rail Online & Strathwood Library Collection

More Jubilee activity at Blackpool Central no doubt in connection with the town's famous illuminations has brought 45578 United Provinces and others here to be stabled beneath the depot's overhead wiring training rig on 29 September 1963. *Strathwood Library Collection*

Two Black Fives flank one of Blackpool's own last surviving Jubilees 45705 Seahorse alongside the shed's sand furnace on 7 March 1964.
Strathwood Library Collection

A recent overhaul at Horwich has given this Aspinall Class 3F 52447 a final lease of life when seen brewing up in the shed yard at Blackpool Central on 22 May 1949. There had been four hundred and sixty-eight of these 0-6-0s built by the Lancashire & Yorkshire Railway, with two hundred and forty-five lasting long enough to join British Railways a year earlier. *Colour Rail*

Opposite: The Lancashire & Yorkshire Railway's outpost at Fleetwood followed the fortunes of its parent shed at Blackpool with regards to shed code changes. Going from 24F to 28B and back to 24F within four years, finally becoming 10C in 1963 to take it into closure on 14 February 1966. Eight of these shortlived Standard Class 2MTs called Fleetwood home at one stage or other, with 84016 behind another one in residence on 2 September 1962. *Rail Online*

Out in the shed yard at Fleetwood on 1 June 1957 it was peaceful onboard the Hughes/Fowler Crab even though it was bounded by a waterworks, repair shops, factories and sidings. *Rail Online*